IMAGES OF ENGLAND

BOURNEMOUTH

IMAGES OF ENGLAND

BOURNEMOUTH

IAN ANDREWS & FRANK HENSON

TEMPUS

Frontispiece: The 'Scotch church' was the popular name for St Andrew's Presbyterian church at the foot of Richmond Hill. Originally it was an iron structure and was rebuilt in 1872. Natwest bank now occupies the site. In 1886 the church transferred to Exeter Road and it recently closed as redundant. This engraving was published by T.J. Hankinson, who came to Bournemouth in 1858 for his health and set up business alongside his home in the Square as a stationer, publisher and estate agent. His Victoria Library lent books to visitors and residents. In 1875 he transferred his business to the foot of Richmond Hill and from 1876 he published the first of many editions of a guide covering Bournemouth, Christchurch, Wimborne and Corfe Castle. From 1876 Bournemouth had limited self-government in the guise of independent commissioners. T.J. Hankinson took part and became chairman. When county borough status was acheived in 1890 he was elected the first mayor of Bournemouth.

First published 2004

Tempus Publishing Limited
The Mill, Brimscombe Port,
Stroud, Gloucestershire, GL5 2QG
www.tempus-publishing.com

© Ian Andrews & Frank Henson, 2004

The right of Ian Andrews & Frank Henson to be identified as the Authors
of this work has been asserted in accordance with the
Copyrights, Designs and Patents Act 1988.

British Library Cataloguing in Publication Data.
A catalogue record for this book is available from the British Library.

ISBN 0 7524 3065 3

Typesetting and origination by Tempus Publishing Limited.
Printed in Great Britain.

Contents

A general view of Bournemouth from Terrace Mount, *c*. 1890. This photograph by W.W. Burnand of Poole shows Southbourne Terrace, the Square and the newly planted Pleasure Gardens, with only the spire of St Peter's church and the tower of Holy Trinity church piercing an uncluttered skyline.

Acknowledgements

Many of the images used are from the authors' own collections but the following have also kindly made photographs available for inclusion in the book: T.C. Ashling, G. Austin of Kitchenhams, B. Bainton, M. Barber, Miss C. Bates, the late S.W. Batting, Beales plc, Mrs B. Best, Bournemouth Natural Science Society, Bournemouth RFC, A. Brayley, A. Brewer, N. Burden, Mrs Burton, D. Cave, R. Clarke, Mrs M. Cobb, M. Colman, Mrs M. Cotterill, Mrs S. Cox, *Daily Echo,* R. Diffey, Miss T. Dower, the late P. Dyson, J. Edgington, G. Elsworth, T. Fancy, Mrs G. Frend, Mrs R. Gawler, Mrs S. Glenagle, Miss Y. Glover, P. Goldsworthy, R. Guttridge, R.J. Harris, the late R.F. Hawker, A. Hawkes, Mrs D. Henson, J. Johnson, Mrs S. Johnson, Miss J. Marsh, J. Mooring Aldridge, Mrs C. Perry, R. Pink, Poole Town Supporters Club, B. Redpath, N. Rigler, Mrs J. Sharp, W. Smith & Sons, K. Standing, H. Taylor, the late R. Terrell, Mrs H. Thorby, P. Toms, P. Trayler, H. Tuck & Sons, Miss W. Vernon-Browne, Victoria Press, M. Vincent, D. Warren, J.A. Young.

In addition, grateful thanks to the staff at Bournemouth Heritage Centre at the Triangle, Poole Local Studies Centre, Waterfront, Poole and Dorset County Record Office, Dorchester for their patient assistance.

Introduction

Bournemouth has grown rapidly and relatively recently out of heath land waste on a coast originally frequented only by fisher folk and smugglers and crossed by a few sandy tracks that served travellers between its older and well established neighbours, Poole and Christchurch. It has filled the gap between them and become built up, right up to its boundaries, in little more than a hundred years. In this time it has earned its own separate identity that is visually explored in this book. What is more remarkable is that the life of the town very nearly coincides with the history of the camera.

Look first at the town name. It first appeared as La Bournemowthe 600 years ago when a monk described the location of a stranded whale, at the mouth of a bourne or stream, The area was known as Bourne Mouth in one form or another for the next 450 years – a far cry from the modern spoken 'Bormuth' or the road sign abbreviations seen today of B'mth.

It would have remained sandy heath, scrub, gorse and heather, with some meadow and woodland, incapable of development right up to the sea but for the Christchurch Enclosure Act of 1802 under which the 5,000 acres of the wasteland of the 7,000 acre Liberty of Westover were allotted or sold in lieu of common rights, with the intention of improving agriculture and food production. A handful of major landowners emerged, controlling between them well over half the area – Sir George Ivison Tapps (later with the names Gervis/Meyrick), William Dean (Littledown Estate and Cooper Dean), the Earl of Malmesbury (family name Harris), William Driver (later sold to William Bruce and later Talbot) and Philip Norris (later sold to Sir Percy Shelley). Separately, but then being in Kinson in Dorset, the Talbot family had bought a landholding. In fairness development was not then in mind but income was envisaged from the planting of fir and Scots Pine trees.

The idea that one day in 1810 Lewis Tregonwell's wife, on a day visit, declared she would like a dwelling here, and the town was born, as celebrated in a 'centenary' in 1910 is totally phoney but was a brilliant piece of 'spin' concocted to drum up visitors to the town which has always needed to feed its lifeblood economy after a disastrously bad season in 1909.

Important in the growth of the town were its notable founding families whose ownership thrust them into prominence once the dubious health-giving qualities of the indigenous pines were proclaimed and it became known as 'Montpelier on the South Coast'. There were doctors, businessmen, hoteliers and tradesmen whose services were in demand and the leaders, architects, planners and municipal commissioners who implemented the grand schemes that enhance this sedate watering place. Later there were those who steered the town to accommodate mass travel via the railway, which following initial opposition came late to Bournemouth compared to other resorts. Later still came the motorcar and the coach and ideas of an annual holiday instead of just spas and health cures for the affluent.

Comparisons with Poole and Christchurch are inevitable. The rapid physical growth of the infant Bournemouth was only possible because of the ready availability of labour, services and materials such as bricks and timber supplied or manufactured in these two older towns and utilising their existing communication links with the outside world.

The name of Bournemouth is now known worldwide, not least because of its language schools, and is often adopted abroad as a shorthand to recognition of their place of residence by those actually coming from nearby places. The international airport is in Christchurch and the university's main campus is in Poole as is the home of the orchestra bearing the town's name. The Revd Arthur Hopkinson of St Augustin's, Cemetery Junction, was prophetic when he wrote in 1942 that the 'really wealthy folk have left Bournemouth and are living.... at Branksome, Parkstone and the Sandbanks neighbourhood'. His discovery of 'poverty in the handsome houses' of the 'Queen of watering places' was shocking, but balanced by his belief that 'no English town gives more voluntary work in good causes'.

Over the years the view has occasionally been expressed that there should be an amalgamation to form 'Wessex City', but every mention of this in the past has provoked great hostility. The fact that one can drive straight through three towns without a gap to separate them proves nothing and it does not take a resident long to realise that each town has a distinct personality, different history and unique characteristics.

In the selection of photographs for this book the authors have tried in the main to choose for this volume previously unpublished photographs and provide a wider view of the town than that presented by the more familiar old postcard sources. In this way it can be shown that 'industry' in Bournemouth meant service and not smoke stacks or engineering, that the artisan houses and council estates were built at the back of the town, away from the visitors' view, and that this governed the public transport network, as it was necessary to get these residents to and from work. The photographs are many and various and often taken by amateurs rather than studio photographers.

Ian Andrews and Frank Henson
July 2004

one

A Trip Round
the Borough

Seamoor Road, Westbourne, *c*. 1900. Joseph Medley's sign advertises the wicker and basketwork furniture that was popular at the turn of the twentieth century. He also had premises in Poole Road, Westbourne. E.J. Thompson, wine and spirit merchant and agent for Eldridge Pope, the Dorchester brewers, also ran the post office, which is now at 10 Seamoor Road. The Hogshead public house now occupies the site at the corner of Alumhurst Road.

A busy day in Poole Road, Westbourne, in the 1950s. Jill Mason's on the left was a ladies' gown shop and the premises of house furnishers M. & G. Jacobs was later occupied by a branch of F.W. Woolworth's. The Tea Cosy café on the right was popular with both local workers and shoppers. Eastman's was one of three cleaners in this short shopping parade.

An aerial view of West Howe industrial estate in the early 1930s showing Elliott's and Burden's brickworks in the middle of the picture. Both firms used local clay for their products and most of the surrounding area was still agricultural smallholdings at this time.

The Bear Cross Inn, previously known as The Old Inn, at the junction of the roads leading to Poole, Wimborne, Kinson and Longham, in 1907. The licensee was Francis Lane. The present pub building replaced the original inn in 1931.

Millham's Lane, Kinson, *c.* 1910. This lane was very low lying and was often flooded as can be seen in the picture. Pedestrians had to use the footbridge over the ford that ran to the River Stour at Longham. In the background is St Andrew's church, the oldest church in Bournemouth, also known locally as the smugglers' church.

The Dolphin Inn, Kinson in 1905. This inn has a long history; it may have been a coaching inn during the eighteenth century. In the latter part of the twentieth century many of the larger farmhouses in the area were demolished including Howe Lodge, built for Isaac Gulliver, one of the most famous smugglers in England.

Kinson stores and post office, seen here in around 1905, sold products such as Nestlé's Milk and Sunlight Soap still familiar to shoppers 100 years later. Part of the sign of the Royal Oak public house can be seen on the right.

Howe Lodge, Wimborne Road, Kinson, was one of the many properties owned by Isaac Gulliver the notorious local smuggler. Gulliver had a gang of over forty men but boasted that he never killed an Excise Officer because of his dislike of violence. The lodge was demolished in 1958 for a road-widening scheme.

Red Hill Tea Gardens on the banks of the River Stour. The gardens were a favourite excursion place for the residents of the town. Red Hill might be a shortening of 'reed' as there were reed beds on low-lying land on the River Stour.

With the rapid growth of the area in the late nineteenth and early twentieth centuries Wimborne Road, Winton, became the local shopping centre. Looking along Wimborne Road towards Moordown, the tram is approaching Banks Corner.

Talbot village, established by the Talbot family with wealth from the sale of a farm on the Portobello Estate in London, was a successful attempt to encourage Victorian virtues of self-help and self-sufficiency. The cottages, in vernacular style, had enough land for growing vegetables and flowers and to keep a domestic pig or cow, and surrounding land was let as farms.

Meyrick Park in its early days, *c.* 1898. It was opened in 1894, the ground having been donated to the town by the Meyrick family. Of the 118-acre park, nearly half was developed as the first municipally owned golf course in the country.

Bournemouth cemetery was laid out on 22 acres of land purchased from William Clapcott Dean. The chapel, designed by Christopher Crabbe Creeke, the Bournemouth Commissioners' surveyor, was built in 1877 and consecrated by the Bishop of Winchester in 1878. The non-conformist ground was dedicated three days later. The Roman Catholic part of the grounds was not opened until 1886.

Throop Weir in the early 1940s. This stretch of the River Stour is a popular angling area, well known for trout and salmon. The salmon leap is on the far left of the picture and the line of the river was altered in the 1950s.

There has been a mill at Throop for at least 500 years and generations of local inhabitants worked in the building. For a long time the main product was hard tack, an oval-shaped coarse biscuit, baked without salt and kiln dried, supplied to sailing ships at local ports. Until 1939, when a diesel engine was installed a large water wheel on the outside of the building powered the machinery. Electricity, installed in 1960, powered the mill until production ceased in 1974. It is now owned by a trust and is opened to the public several times a year.

Hurn Court, Holdenhurst was built in the eighteenth century for the first Earl of Malmesbury. The composer Handel, Admiral Lord Nelson and Thomas Hardy were among the many famous visitors to this magnificent mansion. Later the building was used as boys' boarding school, Heron Court. The property is now divided into private apartments.

An RAC patrolman, by the his patrol box, directs the traffic across the narrow old bridge over the River Stour at Iford in the late 1930s. The first bridge at Iford was built in the twelfth century and until the completion of Tuckton Bridge in 1882 it was the only crossing over the river to Christchurch. In the background is the new bridge opened in 1933. Today the old bridge can only be used by pedestrians.

Tuckton Bridge in 1905. The toll bridge was built in 1882 to create an easier link to Christchurch. It was bought by Bournemouth Corporation in 1904 to enable trams to be run through to Christchurch. The replacement bridge was one of the earliest reinforced concrete structures in the country and the first trams ran across it in 1905. Tuckton was then a very small farming community of less than 100 people.

The owner of the Jumpers Restaurant, Miss Ethel Le Neve, standing outside the premises, now the Crooked Beams, in the 1930s after it was damaged by a large storm. Miss Le Neve, who ran the restaurant for over forty years, found infamy as the teenage mistress of Dr Crippen, an American who murdered his wife in London in 1910. Crippen and Ethel fled to Antwerp and boarded a liner to America but were arrested as it approached New York, following the first use of radio by the police to apprehend a criminal. They were arrested and tried at the Old Bailey. Crippen was convicted and executed but Ethel was acquitted of complicity in the murder.

Fisherman's Walk, Southbourne, c. 1900. We can assume from the name that this was a route frequented by fishermen to reach their boats on the shore. Poole Bay was a rich source of fish; shoals of mackerel were within easy reach of the shore during the summer and herring, plaice, sea bass and cod were among the other species of fish caught.

Southbourne was an enterprise to create a new resort undertaken by a Dr Compton in the 1880s. It became part of the borough in 1901, and quickly grew from a small village to a residential area. This picture, taken in around 1910 at the junctions of Seabourne Road, Fisherman's Walk and Fisherman's Avenue, shows Alfred Ives' large tearoom that was popular with the holidaymakers staying in the hotels and guesthouses in Southbourne.

The early shopping parade at Seabourne Road, Southbourne, *c.* 1906. The small businesses catered for the growing population of the suburb and many of the customers it seems arrived by bicycle. The junction with Parkwood Road is in the middle of the picture. According to the poster in the newsagent's window one million bachelors in the country wanted wives.

Christchurch Road, Boscombe during the 1920s. With the rapid growth of Boscombe Christchurch Road quickly became a major shopping area catering for all the customers' demands. The shop on the right is one of the many grocers in the parade of shops. Next door, a long forgotten brand of cigarettes is being advertised at the tobacconists.

Looking towards Boscombe Arcade from Sea Road, *c.* 1905. The Royal Arcade in the background was opened in 1893 and was built at a cost of £40,000. It was designed to attract shoppers to Boscombe from the town centre.

Christchurch Road, Boscombe, at the corner of Palmerston Road, c. 1920. Boots were proudly proclaiming that they were the largest retail chemists in the world. A McDonalds restaurant now occupies this site. The Salisbury Hotel was the first part of the development to open in 1890. A. Jones & Sons occupied the shop on the corner of the Arcade until the 1980s.

Gladstone Road, Boscombe, was one of the residential areas built for an expanding population in the late nineteenth to early twentieth centuries. The advertisements in the windows of Snelgar's corner shop suggest that it may have been a garden and pet food supplier and W. Harris, opposite, a newsagent and tobacconist. Gladstone Road also housed some small businesses, including a vehicle body builder, who later branched into motor vehicles and insurance.

Shelley Park in the 1930s. Sir Percy Florence Shelley, the son of the poet Percy Bysshe Shelley, moved to Boscombe Cottage in 1849. He enlarged the house and renamed it Boscombe Manor. The council later bought the house, which contained a theatre, and grounds in 1937.

The Knyveton Road/Christchurch Road junction, c. 1905. The horse and carriages are going up Boscombe Hill towards the local shops, past Linden Hall Hydro (now redeveloped).

Looking along Holdenhurst Road towards the central station from the Lansdowne in 1908. The building on the right is the Metropole Hotel that was bombed in 1943 with the loss of 128 lives. The Wilts and Dorset Bank on the left was later incorporated into Lloyds Bank.

Gervis Road East, off Meyrick Road, seen here at the end of the nineteenth century. The famous Bournemouth pine trees, recommended at the time as a health benefit, still line the road. On the left is a cab drivers' hut where they could rest while waiting for customers.

Looking over Horseshoe Common in the early 1870s. A twelve-acre area of land was acquired as open space in the 1890s. Holy Trinity church, seen to the right of the picture, was built in 1868 and a tower was added in 1878. Because of falling congregations the church held its last service on 26 October 1973. The building was converted to a medieval banqueting hall called King Arthur's Court but was destroyed in March 1979 in one of the largest fires seen in Bournemouth in recent years.

The 'Golly' advertising sign visible on the corner of the Triangle and Commercial Road in 1964 was a feature of this shop wall for many years, and will be remembered by many people who were children at the time. It was illuminated at night.

Commercial Road seen from St Michael's Rise (now Road) towards the Triangle in around 1900. The photograph was taken outside T.J. Powell's the stationers (on the left), a business that survived until the 1990s. Wareham, the butcher (full name Wareham and Dale), had nine shops in Bournemouth. More recently this shop housed Tandy Electronics but this has now closed. Also in the road were other everyday shops: dairy, hairdresser, wine merchant, fruiterer, the 'below wardrobe dealer', Mrs Watson, two boot makers, chemist and a china and glass shop. All these have now gone. Until 2002 a C & A multiple store traded from redeveloped premises on the right.

Poole Hill, Commercial Road in around 1910, with the shop of Pars & Co. which was one of the first chemist's shops in Bournemouth, dominating the corner at 2 Poole Hill. The tramlines in the middle of the carriageway went around to Avenue Road.

two

Amusement

Bournemouth, unlike other seaside towns, had a team of ponies rather than donkeys for young visitors to ride. The ponies worked in turns and are seen here enjoying a rest before resuming their duties.

Happy holidaymakers ready to start their ride on the ponies at Boscombe pier in the 1950s. The 9d toll would be 4p in today's coinage.

Generations of residents and visitors have enjoyed the open-air concerts at the bandstand in the Lower Gardens. Originally the Bournemouth Municipal Orchestra played in concerts outside the first Winter Gardens.

Members of the public taking the opportunity to observe the progress on the new Beales premises in 1931. The Art Deco design building caused great interest and passers by took risks standing on the surrounding safety fence to watch the contractors at work. The crane in the background was from A.G. Brixey & Sons of Fancy Road, Parkstone.

Five teenagers taking a rest from skating at the Westover Ice Rink in front of an Alpine backdrop. One of the compilers of this book, who considered himself fit, woke up the day after his first effort on ice with aches in muscles he did not know he possessed.

The Punch & Judy show has been a traditional part of the British seaside holiday for generations. This attentive audience must have been photographed in around 1945 as the wartime anti-invasion defences are visible in the sea.

Boscombe Silver Band leads a parade of South African Second World War veterans past the Royal Bath Hotel in March 1949. The band was formed in 1912 as the Boscombe Temperance Band and founder member Jack Webber won a silver medal for his playing in a band contest. The band made two broadcasts in 1939 and was much in demand at local concerts until it folded sometime in the 1950s.

Southbourne Silver Band at the Bandstand at Fisherman's Walk soon after it was formed in 1925. The conductor was Charles Toogood, formerly of the Pokesdown Salvation band; many local bandsmen started their playing with the Citadel bands. Unusually for a silver band there are two clarinets in the line up.

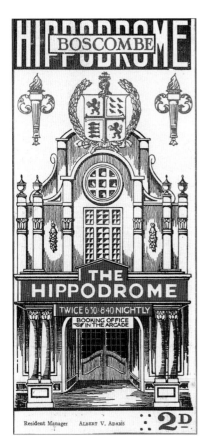

Left: Boscombe Hippodrome opened in 1895 at a cost of £16,000 and was called the Grand Pavilion Theatre and later the Boscombe Theatre. For over sixty years it was a popular venue and many top stars appeared on the bill. In the 1960s it was converted into a dance hall with the Bill Collins Orchestra resident there three nights a week. It is now a nightclub.

Below: Long queues of patrons outside the cinema waiting for the next performance was a familiar sight when popular films were being shown until the 1950s. The original Electric Theatre, Commercial Road, was opened in 1910 and due to the rapidly increasing popularity of cinemas at the time was rebuilt in 1921 to hold 1,400 customers. This picture, taken in the early 1920s, is from the collection of the late Peter Dyson, a well-known local cinema enthusiast.

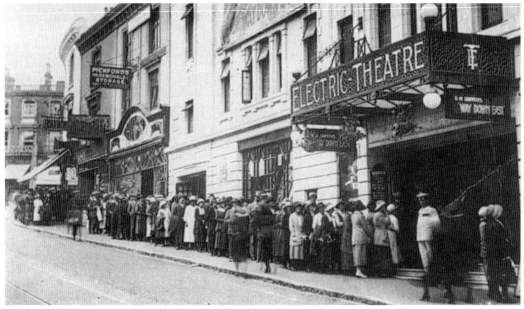

In the carefree summers before the war, the Pier Approach baths hosted a two-hour aquatic revue put together by Roy Fransen, a champion high diver. Local lady swimmers became the graceful Aquabelles, performing synchronised manoeuvres, while double divers plunged into their midst. Slapstick comedy was provided by the Aquabats. Over 100,000 visitors enjoyed the glamour, thrills and comedy each season.

Bournemouth Racecourse at Ensbury Park was a short-lived venture. Racing under National Hunt rules (steeple chasing), for which Southern Railway laid on special excursion trains, only took place there in 1925 and 1926, although there were other meetings in 1927 and 1928. In 1927 it was converted to an aerodrome and air race meeting was held there at Easter 1927. When the area was eventually developed for housing, Western Avenue and Leybourne Avenue were built on the site.

BOURNEMOUTH ELECTRIC THEATRE

PRESENTS

"MONS"

THE HISTORY OF THE IMMORTAL RETREAT

BY PERMISSION OF
HIS MAJESTY'S ARMY COUNCIL

BET   UNQUESTIONABLY THE PREMIER
HOUSE OF ENTERTAINMENT   **BET**

The cover of The Electric Theatre programme, October 1925, for a silent movie portraying the battle of Mons in 1915. There were fifteen musicians in the theatre orchestra and for this film an extra trumpeter was in the pit to perform at special moments in the performance.

three
Military

A ceremony of presenting the colours to the 7th Hants Regiment took place at Meyrick Park in September 1909. Most of the soldiers came from the Bournemouth area.

The Home Fleet of the Royal Navy paid a five-day visit to Poole Bay off the pier in July 1907. Britain had the largest navy in the world during the early 1900s and the visit drew crowds of sightseers to the town with the pier offering a good view of the ships. The mayor, George Edward Bridge, and the councillors entertained the officers of the fleet to a civic luncheon at the Winter Gardens.

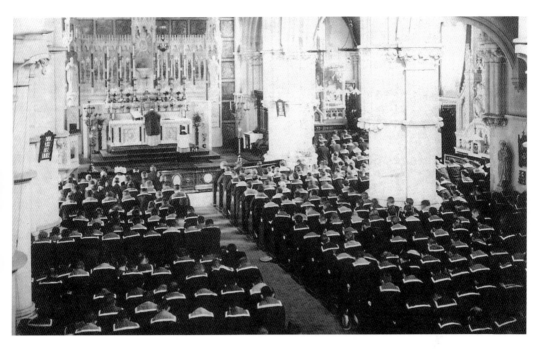

Members of the crews of the ships of the Home Fleet attended a mass at St Peter's church during their visit to the town in July 1907.

Families and well-wishers gathered at the Drill Hall in Holdenhurst Road on 9 August 1914 as members of the 7th Hants Regiment waited anxiously for their orders, just five days after the declaration of war with Germany.

Captain A. Allen of the 7th Hants Regiment passing the junction of Wootton Gardens and Old Christchurch Road. The posters on the wall are advertising a wide variety of entertainment on offer at the time, as well as stores and products.

After receiving their orders members of the 7th Hants Regiment congregated at Bournemouth central station to embark, with their horses, for their destinations, with a large crowd of well-wishers to see them off.

Members of the Lancashire Fusiliers undertook a recruiting campaign through the Square in April 1915. It quickly became obvious that a lot more soldiers were needed and even skilled men were urged to enlist in the forces. Conscription had still not then been introduced.

The mayor, Alderman James Druitt, had been town clerk between 1890 and 1902 and came from a family of lawyers with strong connections with public life in Christchurch. He was a keen supporter of the Volunteer and Territorial Forces and led the 1915 recruiting campaign. Many young, sometimes under-aged, boys volunteered to join the forces. The monocled, elderly officer saluting may well have been a veteran of the Boer War.

The Royal Welsh Fusiliers in 1915 billetted many soldiers in comfortable beds in Moordown, after suffering terrible experiences training on Salisbury Plain. They are pictured near the shop of Walter N. Ridout in Alma Road, on their way to the rifle ranges at Winton Recreation Ground. The regiment suffered many losses later, but some survivors came back to marry Moordown girls.

The 3rd Battalion of the Hampshire Regiment marching along Christchurch Road, Boscombe, during the First World War. The Freemantle post office survived into the early twenty-first century. The local name of Freemantle for this area of Boscombe is now little used.

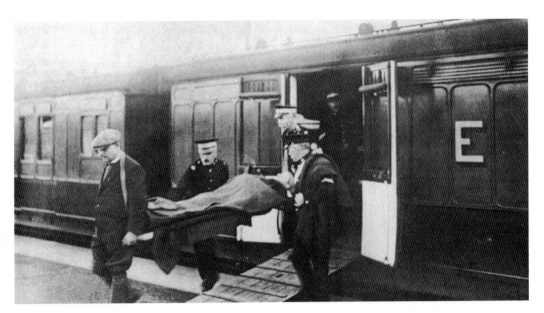

Wounded First World War soldiers being taken off an ambulance train, probably at Boscombe station, on the way to local hospitals or one of many large houses used as temporary nursing homes. To disguise the numbers of wounded and the extent of their injuries from public view this task was often carried out at night. As many as 400 wounded soldiers were received here in three weeks after the Battle of the Somme in 1916.

This Bournemouth Model Laundry van was used as a temporary ambulance to transport seriously wounded soldiers who had been evacuated from the battlefront in October 1916. At that time there were ten ambulances operating, five of them converted from local tradesmen's vans. This stretcher case is being loaded into the vehicle by members of St John's Ambulance.

Above: After the First World War many returning ex-servicemen found employment with the expanding local council departments. Bournemouth Tramways employed over 300 staff in 1924 and in this group photograph many of them are proudly wearing their military decorations.

Left: Beales was one of the many tall building used as anti-aircraft positions during the Second World War.

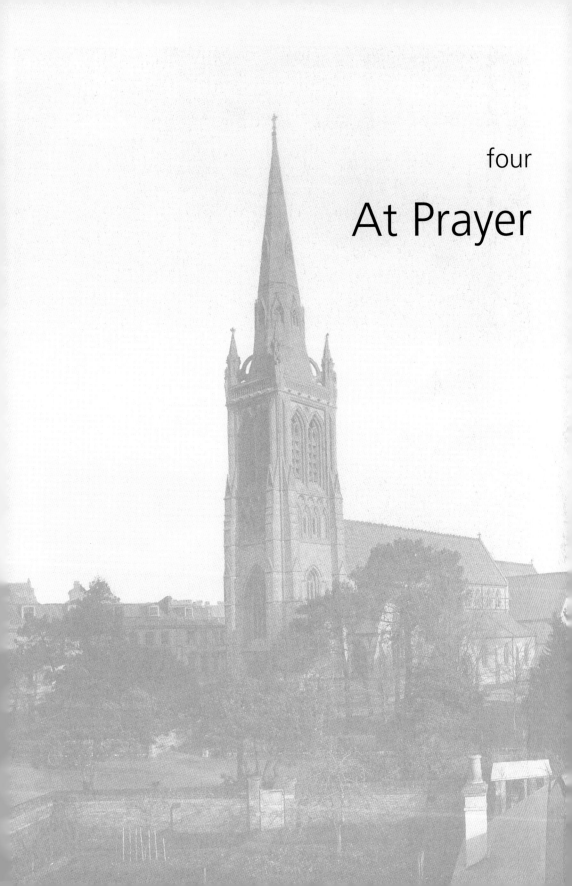

four

At Prayer

Left: An unusual, late nineteenth-century view of St Peter's church, showing in the foreground the rear gardens of nos 1 and 2 Westover Villas, now redeveloped as Austin Reed's shop. The first church, which had a tower, and no spire, was founded in the 1840s in the wake of the Oxford Movement – Evangelical worshippers were later happier to worship at Holy Trinity. The architect of the present church was George Street (who also designed the Law Courts in London's Strand). The heart of Percy Bysshe Shelley, the poet, is buried in a family tomb in the church.

Until 1861 when they could attend a convent chapel, Roman Catholics in Bournemouth had to travel to Poole for worship. The Oratory of the Sacred Heart opened in 1875 (and extended in 1900) was in a central position on Richmond Hill to serve their needs. It was at this church in the late 1890s that controversial artist and writer Aubrey Beardsley converted to the Roman Catholic Church. This photograph was taken in around 1930; the scaffolding on the left shows the present *Daily Echo* offices under construction. To the right of the Sacred Heart was the Gothic-style Methodist Punshon Memorial Church, demolished by enemy bombs in 1943.

Another church designed by George Street was the simple Dutch barn–like St Michael and All Angels – not the present building now in St Michael's Road, but a predecessor on the site of the Devon Towers Hotel, here photographed by Bournemouth's first photographer, Robert Day, sometime between 1866 and 1876.

The Talbot sisters, spinsters Georgina and Mary Anne, inherited a fortune from the sale of the Portobello Farm Estate in Kensington and applied it to creating a model community. Its church, consecrated in 1870, the date of this photograph, was built on the highest land in the area. It now serves as the parish church of Wallisdown, and was imaginatively enlarged in 1985, using roof trusses crafted by Ken Latham in a Poole boatyard.

Boscombe Baptist church built in 1874 was partnered by one at the Lansdowne in 1875. Both were built by the efforts of local Baptists to cater for their needs in a then still growing area, as well as for holiday visitors. Their members were widely spread across the borough and previously met in homes or hired accommodation. When £1,200 had been collected (enough to build one chapel) the foundation stone at Boscombe was laid and work was started.

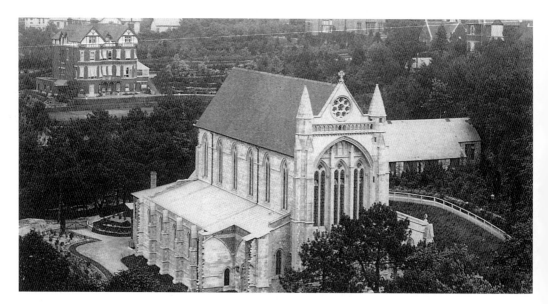

A postcard view from around 1900 of the well-proportioned St Stephen's church, designed by John Pearson in 1881 and seen here before the construction of its distinctive tower in 1907. A spire was also intended, but the money ran out. Sir John Betjeman called it the most beautiful building in the town and one of the finest examples of Victorian church architecture in the country.

five

At Work

Left: A blacksmith's shop at Pokesdown (on the site of the present station entrance), *c.* 1905. The blacksmiths and farriers were important tradesmen before motor vehicles replaced horses as the main mode of transport. In 1935 there were still nine blacksmiths in Bournemouth.

Below: The baker's delivery van was a familiar sight until after the Second World War. Bread was made for years in wood or coal ovens, but 'electric machines', as used by L.E. King of Holdenhurst Road, allowed a consistent loaf to be produced in quantity, starting the decline of small traditional bakers. The standard loaf was white and made of unenriched wheatgrain, rather than wholemeal. After about 1930 such loaves were also available pre-sliced by machine.

Above: Tom Luther (left), his son Dennis (bending down), with an unknown helper digging up turnips and swedes at the family smallholding behind St Mark's church, Talbot Village during the 1930s. There were many small farms on the outskirts of the town, some surviving until the 1980s. Talbot Village had been founded by the Misses Talbot as a model community with land for cultivation attached to each property to encourage self-sufficiency.

Below: The staff and family of Marshall & Bower the builders of no. 57 Elmes Road, Winton, photographed outside their workshop in the 1920s. The corrugated iron workshop was typical of the small business premises of that era – not expensive to build but very cold to work in during the winter. The firm later changed its name to Marshall Pascoe.

Haulage contractor Harry Tuck and his employees stand in the yard next to a new Super Sentinel Three Way Tipper (DG4T model) purchased in 1920 at a cost of £927 10s 0d. It was the first motor wagon bought by the firm. The company is still at the same address in Midland Road, Winton, and the firm is now run by Harry's grandsons.

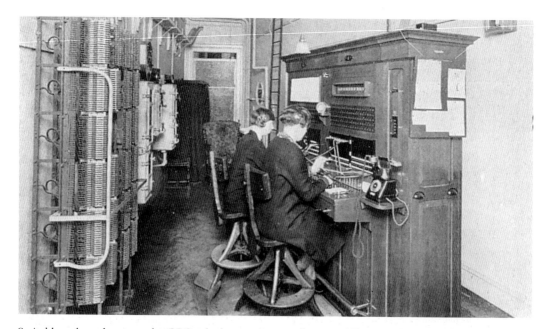

Switchboard employees at the GPO telephone private exchange at The Royal Bath Hotel in the 1920s. The Royal Bath boasted that there was a telephone in every room as befitted a hotel of the highest standard.

Right: Doris Crabb of Newtown, Poole, a Southern Railways goods deliverer in the late 1930s, is seen here with 'Bonnie' who pulled the wagon. During the Second World War Miss Crabb qualified as a passenger train guard and worked on the Bournemouth-Salisbury-Waterloo route.

Below: F.W. Woolworth's café on the first floor of the extended shop in The Square in 1939. The café manageress was Mrs Maud Budge and amongst the staff was her younger sister Barbara (fourth from left). Among the salads offered were boiled ham, fresh salmon, egg mayonnaise and ham, veal and egg pie, all at 6d. Ham rolls were 2d. The store also had a snack bar and an ice cream and soda fountain counter.

During the postal strike of 1962 local solicitors formed their own local and inter-town collection and delivery system. The Bournemouth document exchange centre was in the offices of Mooring Aldridge and Haydon at Westover Chambers, Hinton Road. The system was designed to enable solicitors to keep important transactions going for the duration of a dispute that went on for several weeks, but was so efficient it became a more permanent service.

It is difficult to imagine from this idyllic scene taken near Littledown in Castle Lane in June 1939 that Britain was very soon to be at war. The photographer was the late Harry Ashley who became chief photographer at the *Evening Echo* after war service.

six

Sport

Members of the Sharland family, who owned the Tralee Hotel, St Michaels Road, and their guests, enjoy a game of croquet on the lawn at the rear of the hotel in the 1880s. Croquet was one of the few sports that was considered suitable for ladies to play and many larger houses and hotels had a croquet lawn at the time.

A runner in the 1910 Bournemouth Marathon, accompanied by race officials from the cycling section of the Bournemouth Athletics Club, near the finishing line in the Square. The twenty-one competitors travelled by train to Brockenhurst and raced the eighteen and a half miles back to Bournemouth. The winner was F.W. Webber. The prize for his efforts was the princely sum of two guineas and he got to keep the prize cup as well as he had also won the race in the previous two years.

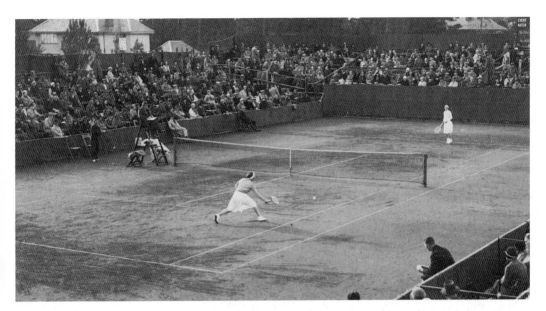

The opening game of the 1933 British Hard Court Tennis Championship Ladies Single Final at the West Hants Tennis Club between Miss Helen Jacobs of the USA (nearest the camera) and Miss Dorothy Round of the United Kingdom. Miss Round went on to win by 3-6, 6-2, 6-3 and she retained the title in 1934. She also won the Wimbledon Ladies' title twice. This championship was one of the top events of the year and most of the top players competed in it.

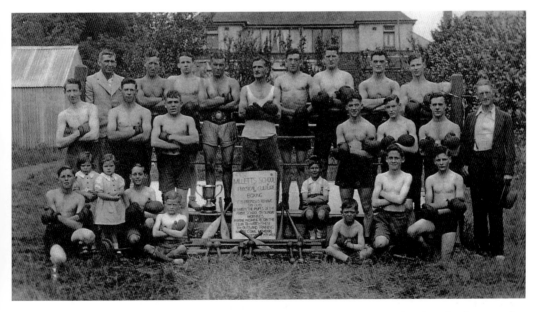

The Milletts School of Boxing was based at Glenville Road, Ensbury Park. The school arranged training and practice bouts for boxing hopefuls on Sunday mornings for a subscription of a few pence a week. The boxer in the back row of this 1935 photograph, wearing a championship belt, was local champion Ted Sherwood who had over 360 fights, winning most of them. He was a popular fighter all over the country.

A football game at the Saugeen School, Derby Road, in 1908. Hooped shirts were a usual feature of school sports kit from the late 1800s.

A crucial football match was played between Boscombe and Poole Town at Kings Park on 6 April 1907. Boscombe won by two goals to nil. The victory secured Boscombe the Hants League Western Division championship. Boscombe football club was formed from Boscombe St John's Lad's Institute team. When they were admitted to the Football League in 1923 the club's name was changed to Bournemouth & Boscombe Athletic FC.

J.E. Beale's ladies hockey team in 1920-21. Beale's, like many companies, encouraged their employees in social and sporting activities and it was considered an honour to represent the company. Unfortunately Beale's sometimes had difficulty fielding their strongest teams as Bealson's (their associated store) half day was on Wednesday and Beale's was on Saturday when most games were played.

Cllr Harry Mears, the deputy mayor, presenting the prizes for an open angling competition held on Bournemouth beach 17 April 1955. The event was organised by Bournemouth Gas sea angling club and the profit from the competition was donated to the Guide Dogs for the Blind Association. Out of the 410 anglers that took part only about forty-eight caught fish. On the right in the background is local angling correspondent Derek Fletcher who later wrote for the *Daily Telegraph*. Mr Binney of the Guide Dogs for the Blind is in the middle at the back.

Bournemouth Swimming Club was founded from an 'Early Bathers Association', Premier Rowing Club who played 'aquatic handball' (better known now as water polo) in the sea from at least 1876. The club's heyday was in the 1930s when its ladies' team was the best in the land, led by Olive Wadham, twelve times ASA 100 yards champion, competitor in the first Empire Games in Canada in 1930 and chosen to represent Great Britain in the famous 1936 Olympics in Berlin. As far as we have been able to establish Bournemouth's only Olympic competitor. Olive (née Joynes) is pictured here in 1932 on the left. Other swimmers, left to right, are Ethel Pascall, Yvonne Glover, Ruth Cooper and Mrs Miles.

A very early picture of the Bournemouth YMCA Boating Club that was the forerunner of the Bournemouth Rowing Club.

LIBERATION OF PIGEONS AT BOURNEMOUTH.

Releasing homing pigeons at a Bournemouth railway siding in the 1930s. The birds were sent to Bournemouth from the Midlands and North of England and when the weather conditions were right they were released for their flight home. The spire of St Paul's church can be seen in the background.

Indoor bowling was a popular activity in the Winter Gardens in the 1930s. During the winter weather when outdoor bowling was impossible players could enjoy the sport in comfort. Judging by the size of the crowd this could have been a championship final.

An action photograph taken during the Chamber of Trade bowling cup competition in 1923, during the presidency of W.W. Graham of Hants and Dorset Motor Services. Today's players would observe a stricter dress code, but little else seems to have changed. The first council Bowling Green was at Meyrick Park using the croquet lawn. Previously the game had been played on the tennis courts.

A 1930s class of the Women's League of Health and Beauty that met in St Stephen's Hall, usually on Monday evenings. Mrs Mary Bagot-Stack founded the league in 1930 and Molly Brown and her sister Madge led the Bournemouth classes. The organisation was renamed The Fitness League in 1999.

seven

Shopping

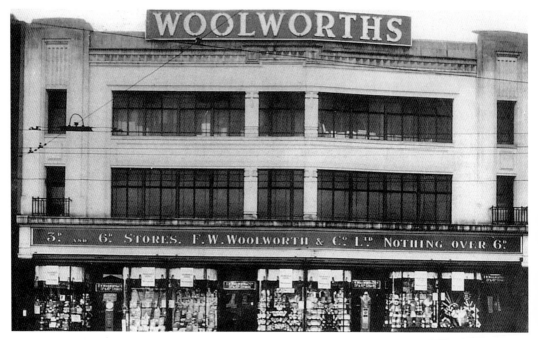

Woolworths' 3d and 6d shop in The Square in 1939, soon after it was extended. Over 200,000 tons of soil were removed from the rear to enlarge the store. The shop had two thirds of a mile of counter space and employed more than 250 staff.

John Phillips, a fellow of The Royal Horticultural Society, had a large nursery and greengrocer's shop at the junction of Seamoor Road and Middle Road, now Robert Louis Stevenson Avenue, Westbourne. In those days a nursery could supply labour as well as goods. In 1913 he charged four shillings a day for his employees to work for customers in their own gardens and to have a load of rubbish cleared was two shillings.

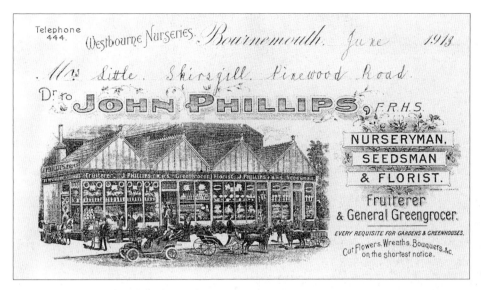

The predecessor of the garden centre. An elaborate billhead of John Phillips shows the size of the firm's extensive premises in Seamoor Road – more impressive than an inch of till roll! Mr Phillips was the proud recipient of a letter from King George V when his four sons all volunteered for military service in 1914. The shop was one of the largest in Westbourne before the First World War.

The corner of Gervis Place and Westover Road in around 1938, showing a Belisha beacon and overhead trolleybus cables. Austin Reed Ltd, military and civilian tailors and outfitters, still occupy the same shop. Among the shops in Gervis Place was the shoe shop of A. Jones & Sons, who also had a shop in the Boscombe Arcade. Westover Road used to be the 'Bond Street' of Bournemouth.

Robinson & Williams ironmonger's stores on Poole Hill in 1911. The shop stocked a large range of goods for the house and garden. They were also painters and decorators, employing workers to fulfil outside contracts.

Bournemouth Arcade as it looked in 1908. This arcade was built by Henry Joy in 1866 and was considered by many as a 'white elephant' when it was opened. Frederick Bright opened a needlework shop in the Arcade in 1871 that was later developed by his son Percy into the large department store now known as Dingles.

Inside the arcade in 1906, by which time it had become a popular shopping area. The shop advertising cigars (Offer's) was well patronised by the authors. It continued as a tobacconists until the 1970s and stocked hand-rolled cigars, a wide variety of pipe tobaccos and scented snuff.

Old Christchurch Road, *c.* 1914. By this date many stores had opened in the road establishing it as a more high-class shopping area than Commercial Road and Poole Hill.

Leverett & Frye, grocers and provision suppliers, in The Square, *c.* 1908. The Bournemouth branch was part of a chain of eleven shops, mainly in the London area. The premises were later rebuilt as Forte's Café and ice-cream parlour. Today it is pub in the J.D. Wetherspoon's chain called Moon In The Square.

While the bomb-damaged store at Old Christchurch Road was being rebuilt in the early 1950s Beales moved to premises near the corner of Fir Vale Road. Outside this shop is seen here a Beales delivery van; their fleet of distinctive brown and cream vehicles was a familiar sight in the town.

Harvey Nichols

An advertisement for Harvey Nichols & Co. Ltd on Commercial Road, Bournemouth
from *Residential Bournemouth*.

Beales opened a temporary shop at nos 40-42 Christchurch Road after the bombing raid of 23 May 1943 destroyed the original premises. J.E. Beale came to Bournemouth from Weymouth to open his first shop at St Peter's Terrace in 1881. The company expanded by taking over surrounding premises as they became available and a large new department store was built in 1931 on the site.

Farrah's Meat Market on the corner of Gladstone Road and Portman Road, Boscombe. Farrah's shop was on this site for about fifty years serving the public and catering for the local guesthouse trade. After the firm closed the building was used as a bedding store. Note the elegant brackets carrying the power lines for the trams that passed the door.

The cycle shop of J.H.G. Tolhurst in the parade of local shops at Wallisdown Road in the 1940s. All the bikes on sale are the upright and sturdy type that could be supplied in either free wheel, or three speed gear models. Mr Tolhurst, known to most as John, always wore Oxford bags and was also a model aeroplane enthusiast. Today an Aldi supermarket is on the site.

Opposite below: Beales Stationery Department's products took up ten pages of its 1907 shop catalogue and included thirty-five different types of notepaper for sale. Customer's names and addresses were embossed on the notepaper for no extra charge. A cut die for an address cost 2s and 6d. The store acquired the distinctive telephone number Bournemouth no. 1 by exchanging with a Westbourne shop and reprinting its stationery free of charge. They used a rubber stamp to make the change on their own stationery stock.

Parkstone & Bournemouth Co-operative Society's shop on the corner of Spring Road and Cleveland Road was built in 1917. The Co-op was popular with its customers who shared in the organisation's profits by receiving a dividend on the money they spent. The headquarters of the society was at Longfleet House, Parkstone Road, Poole.

W.H. Goldsworthy's bakery and tea rooms were at 688 Christchurch Road, Boscombe. Bread and cakes were baked at their own bakery behind the shop in Haviland Road, called The Golden Grain Bakery. The business also provided a home delivery service over a wide area including Christchurch.

eight

Services

THE SQUARE, BOURNEMOUTH. 38.

BOURNEMOUTH GAS UNDERTAKING

Opposite above: An Advance Linen Service van turns into Bourne Avenue from the Square, *c.* 1955. Laundry services were, and still are, very important to Bournemouth, a town full of hotels and guesthouses. In 1950 there were seventeen laundries in the town.

Opposite below: After nationalisation of the gas companies in 1949, Bournemouth Gas & Water Company's showrooms and head office were at 134 −136 Old Christchurch Road. The Bournemouth Water Co. offices had moved to 144 Old Christchurch Road. Before the separation of the two services the company had over 1,300 employees.

Right: The water tower at Meyrick Park in 1900. Bournemouth's rapid growth had necessitated that a good water supply and head of water was provided to maintain efficient supplies. This tower was the first ferro-concrete water tower in the country.

Below: The saying, 'hard work never killed anyone' was put rigorously to the test as workmen struggled to lay power lines under the Tuckton Bridge in the 1920s.

The Central Library at the Lansdowne was opened on 26 March 1913 and occupied the same site until 2003 when the new library was opened at the Triangle. The busts and pictures of famous composers seen here were in the music library at the Lansdowne site.

The Royal Victoria and West Hants Hospital (known locally as Boscombe Hospital) at Ashley Road was built on land purchased from Bournemouth Gas & Water Co. The first wards were opened in 1900 and Princess Alexandra (daughter of King Edward VII) opened extra wards in 1902. With the building of the new hospital at Littledown the Ashley Road buildings were demolished in 1992 and the site redeveloped for housing.

Ernest Burden House on East Overcliff Drive was a residential home for retired members of the Queen Alexandra Nursing Corps. Many organisations had rest and recuperation homes in Bournemouth, as the sea air was considered beneficial to health. The lady sitting second left in the picture is Bessie Shurben from Poole who was a Queen Alexandra nurse for over twenty years.

Walter Smith began as a carriage maker at Pine Road in 1892 and started an undertaking business after arranging a funeral for a local gypsy. He moved his business, pictured here in 1908, to Wimborne Road, Winton in 1896 where the business still is (now W. Smith & Sons) with a modern frontage added on to the original house.

Before supermarkets started selling milk at discount prices most households had their milk delivered by a local roundsman. Pearce's Dairy was one of the many local suppliers in Bournemouth. Until electric milk floats came into use in the 1950s, most businesses delivered by pony-drawn carts, hand cart or trade bike. When Joe Pearce started his company he delivered milk seven days a week, including Christmas, starting at 5 o'clock in the morning and finishing in late afternoon.

The hotel business has always been the lifeblood of Bournemouth's economy. This picture shows the grandeur of the Garden Dining Room of The Royal Bath Hotel in 1925. The Royal Bath with its commanding position on East Cliff was Bournemouth's first hotel. Bought by Sir Merton Russell-Cotes in 1876 it was owned by members of his family until 1963, when Leslie Jackson bought this five star hotel (less its Victorian paintings) for De Vere's Hotels from Mrs Phyllis Lee Duncan.

nine

Events

Part of Christchurch Road, Boscombe, was closed to traffic on 19 November 1932 to allow a large crowd to watch Father Christmas arrive at the Plummer Roddis at 501 Christchurch Road. When he arrived at the store Father Christmas climbed onto the roof and entered the shop via a large chimney built for the occasion.

J.J. Allen's department store on the corner of Hinton Road and St Peter's Road decorated for the coronation of George VI in May 1937. J.J. Allen was born in Luton in 1857 and came to Bournemouth in 1878. He opened a store in the Arcade with James Worth before moving to the site at Hinton Road. He lived at 'Cerne Abbas', a large residence in The Avenue, Branksome Park. He died while on a visit to Capetown in March 1914.

The staff of the new Winton (Moordown) no. 1 branch of the Parkstone and Bournemouth Co-op in Wimborne Road assemble for the opening day, 10 July 1912. The co-operative movement at the time was 'wishing success' to the lobbying of local shop assistants for a minimum wage for shop workers and by 1918 had affiliated with the local Labour Party. The workers may have been poorly paid but they were elegantly dressed for the occasion.

A proud moment for Bournemouth Football Club (known as the Poppies) was the presentation of a new flag by Mrs E. St John Burton at the club's ground at Victoria Park, Winton on 10 September 1910. Mrs St John Burton, a keen supporter of the club, designed and made the flag. Unfortunately, on the day, the flag did not bring any luck to the club as they lost 6-2 to Cowes.

The 1935 carnival procession in Christchurch Road, Boscombe, approaching the junction with Somerset Road. The Central Studios are advertising Selo film, a brand that was popular between the wars. A contemporary survey described Boscombe as top for sobriety in the country.

The funeral of Mrs Louise Barnes crossing Turbary Common on its way to Kinson church on 25 September 1935. Mrs Barnes was known as the 'Queen of the Gypsies' and had been head of the Romany encampment called Little England at Turbary Common. Her ninety-year-old husband survived her and over seventy direct descendants followed the cortege to the church.

Walking in procession along Old Christchurch Road are some of the 8,000 schoolchildren who took park in The Children's Festival held in Meyrick Park on 23 June 1909. Civic leaders were in the park and altogether over 16,000 people attended the event. The band of the 7th Hants Regiment entertained the crowd and a sports programme was arranged, including three-legged races.

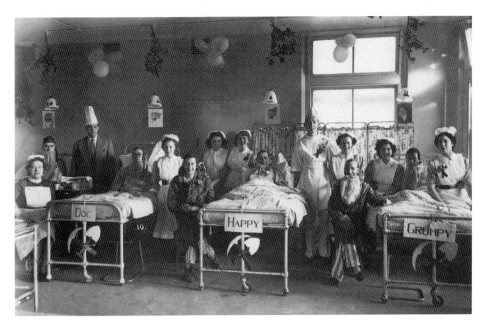

The wards in Bournemouth Victoria Hospital were decorated with different themes for Christmas 1951. Ward 19 chose Snow White and the Seven Dwarfs, and all the patients and staff seem to be enjoying the occasion. Standing to the right of the 'Happy' bed is Peter Traynor, a nurse on the ward.

Above: During the First World War the fate of our continental allies was a matter of concern to the British public and funds were established to assist people of those countries. The French Relief Fund held a flag day in July 1915 when gifts from the public were donated. Anyone giving over ten shillings to the appeal was mentioned in the local press. In the background Bobby & Co. was holding a summer sale.

Right: The historic 58th Trades' Union Congress was held at the town hall in September 1926 in the immediate aftermath of the nine days' General Strike. It was attended by national figures, including ex-Prime Minister Ramsay McDonald, who, with the other leading figures, signed this copy of the programme. Bournemouth was presented as 'The Sunshine City – England's Playground by the Sea'. Much was made of municipal enterprises being in the true spirit of socialism, although, it was said, 'like the British Empire, they were founded in a fit of absence of mind and….had grown up like Topsy without knowing how'.

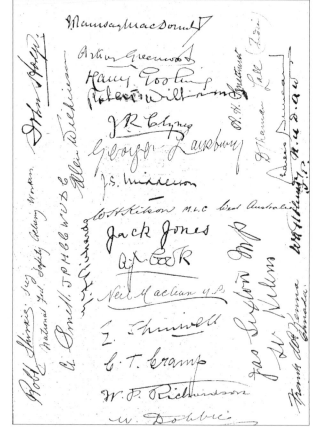

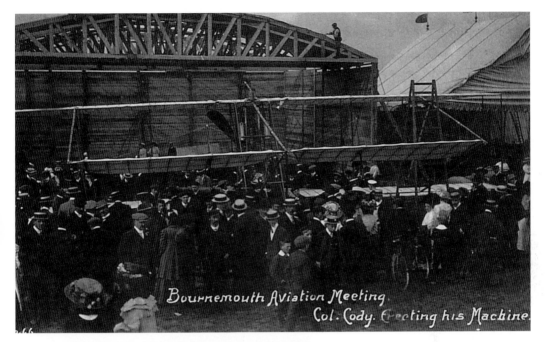

Bournemouth Aviation Meeting
Col. Cody. Erecting his Machine.

Above: Bournemouth was popular with aviation pioneers. This aviation event was to be the Grand Finale of the 1910 Centenary Festival. Aimed at ridding Bournemouth of its staid and stuffy bath chair image, it was the first such international event held in the country, was sponsored by the Royal Aero Club and took place on the cliffs at Southbourne. Texas born, but a naturalized Briton since 1896, Col. Samuel Cody took part. He had built his first flying machine in 1908 and later died in a flying accident in 1913. The event ended with the sort of publicity no one ever wants. The Hon. C.S. Rolls was killed when the tail of his biplane broke and he crashed to the ground on 12 July. This was the first fatal accident to a British pilot.

Left: A number of ideas from the Riviera, including prize silk banners made by artists from Nice, captivated the public at the 1910 festival. Some of the fine banners, recently restored, are now displayed in Bournemouth Town Hall.

A Battle of the Flowers, as in Jersey, Nice and Cannes, was a highlight of the 1910 Centenary. The theme was intended to establish Bournemouth firmly on the international map of quality holiday destinations.

Local politics at the 1910 Festival. This float is a protest about the lack of tram services on Sundays. The pressure continued and in 1913 a Sunday afternoon service was introduced.

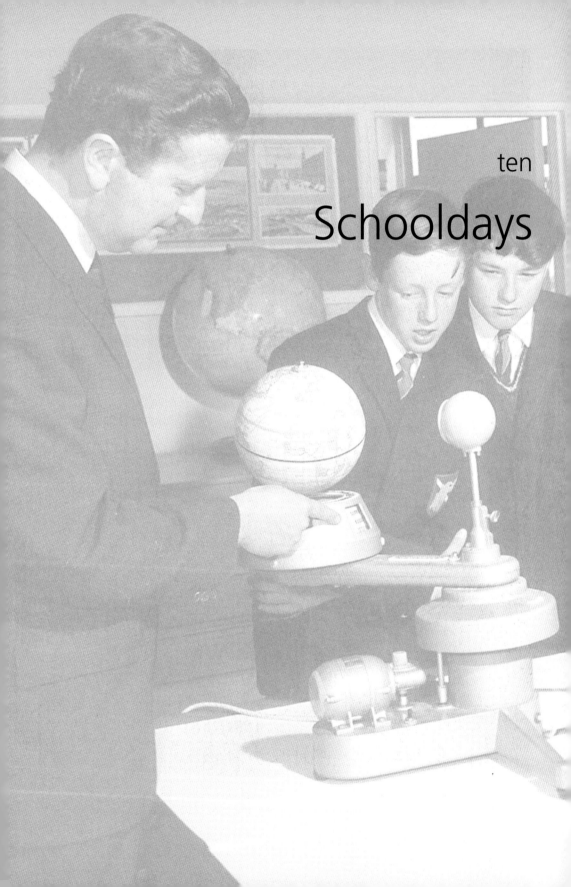

ten

Schooldays

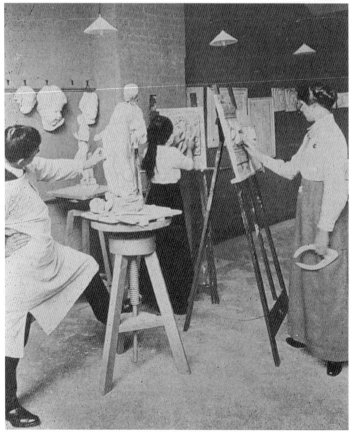

Above: The senior Cricket XI of Bournemouth School for Boys of the 1920s in their distinctive whites. Note the lace-up boots worn at that time.

Left: Bournemouth once had two Schools of Art. There was the Drummond Road School of Art at Boscombe, run on the lines of the Mechanics Institute, and the Bournemouth West School of Art on Poole Hill, the modelling room of which is seen here in around 1902. Bournemouth Education Committee assumed responsibility for both in 1903 and combined the two into the College of Art on a newly acquired site at the Lansdowne in 1909.

The interior of the big schoolroom at Grassendale, Southbourne-on-Sea in 1914. A private girls' school 'cultivating trust, confidence and loyalty' among its pupils occupied these premises between 1888 and 1936. The original building has been enlarged and is now occupied by St Peter's RC school.

When the Revd Morden Bennett became the first vicar of Bournemouth in 1845 he made it a priority to establish a church school. It was eventually built in St Peter's Road in central Bournemouth in 1850 and survived until 1937.

The Officer Training Corps at Portchester Road school on parade in 1915. Founded as a Technical School in 1901, later to be called Bournemouth School, its cadet corps dates from 1903.

St John's Church of England School, Moordown, swimming group in the style of costume appropriate for the date, 1924.

The Guide troop at St John's, Boscombe, in 1928.

Peter Johnson, a geography teacher and deputy headmaster of Oakmead Secondary School demonstrates the Sun Tracker – a device he invented as a teaching aid – to a top class in 1963. The photograph reappeared thirty years later on the cover of a rock album by a group called The Wonder Stuff.

During the night of 16 November 1940 a German landmine exploded at Alma Road infants' school causing the extensive damage seen. In the same raid fifty-three people were killed and many properties were damaged in Malmesbury Road and Robert Louis Stevenson Avenue.

In 1947 the school leaving age was raised to fifteen and additional accommodation had to be provided quickly. Hence a rash of temporary huts appeared in schools in Bournemouth, and all over the country, which are still remembered by many. They were officially known as HORSA huts, short for 'Hut Operation, Raising of School Age'.

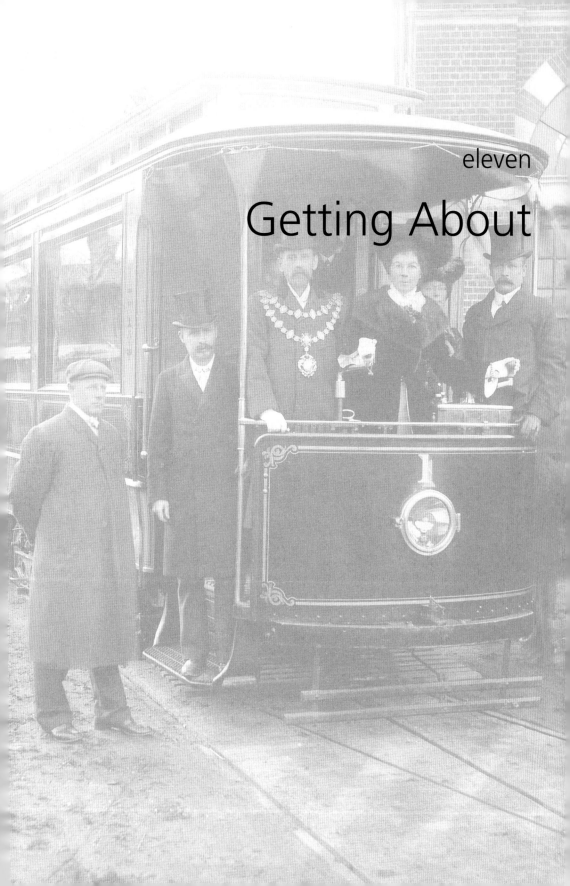

eleven

Getting About

Telephone No. 319.

WEST CLIFF MEWS
NEAR THE HIGHCLIFF HOTEL.

LIST OF PRICES.

LANDAU or BROUGHAM with One Horse.
Including Driver.

	s.	d.
First Hour } within the Borough .... {	3	6
Second Hour	3	0
To Station (according to number of persons and luggage) .... 1/6, 2/-, 2/6 and	3	6
,, Church and back, in the town	3	6
,, St. Clement's or Branksome Church and back	6	6
,, Dinner Party, in town	5	0
,, Ball or Evening Party after 12.0 midnight....	10	6
,, Town Hall or Theatre	5	0
,, Talbot Village and Woods	5	6
,, Throop and Holdenhurst for drive	6	6
,, Boscombe, Pokesdown, Iford, Holdenhurst, Throop and Winton	8	6
,, Southbourne and back	6	6
,, Branksome Chine	5	6
,, Branksome Chine, Canford Cliffs & Haven Hotel	10	0
,, Constitution Hill and Parkstone	6	6
,, Canford Cliffs and Parkstone	8	6
,, Constitution Hill, Parkstone and Branksome Chine	10	0
,, Constitution Hill and Poole	10	0
,, Southbourne and Christchurch	10	0
,, Heron Court and Rhododendron Forest	10	0
,, Canford and Wimborne	18	6
,, Christchurch and Mudeford	12	6
,, Upton House, Hamworthy and Poole	15	0
,, Heron Court, Longham, Kinson (18 miles)....	15	0

DOUBLE BATH CHAIRS.
Including Driver.

	s.	d.
Each hour within the Borough	2	6
To Station .... 1/6 and	2	0
,, Throop and Holdenhurst	5	0
,, Boscombe, Pokesdown, Iford, Holdenhurst, Throop and Winton	6	6
,, Southbourne and back	5	0
,, Branksome Chine and back	5	0
,, Constitution Hill and Parkstone	5	0
,, Branksome Chine, Canford Cliffs & Parkstone	6	6
,, Branksome Chine, Canford Cliffs and Haven Hotel	7	6
,, Constitution Hill, Parkstone & Canford Cliffs	7	6
,, Constitution Hill and Poole	7	6
,, Southbourne and Christchurch	7	6
,, Canford and Wimborne	15	0
,, Christchurch and Mudeford	10	6
,, Heron Court, the Rhododendron Forest	7	6
,, Church and back, in town	3	6
,, St. Clement's or Branksome Church and back	5	0
,, Town Hall or Theatre	3	6
,, Dinner Parties in town	3	6
,, Ball or Evening Party after 12.0 midnight	7	6

LANDAU or OPEN CARRIAGE with Pair Horses.
Including Driver.

	£	s.	d.
To Canford and Wimborne	1	7	6
,, Constitution Hill and Poole	0	15	6
,, Southbourne and Christchurch	0	15	6
,, Corfe Castle	2	2	0
,, New Forest	2	10	0
,, By the Hour—First Hour	0	6	6
Second Hour	0	6	0

PRIVATE OMNIBUSSES.

	£	s.	d.
Private Omnibus to East or West Station	0	6	6
Private Omnibus for Dinner Party	0	10	0
Private Omnibus for Ball or Evening Party after 12.0	1	0	0

BRAKES FOR LARGE OR SMALL PARTIES BY CONTRACT.

HORSES TAKEN IN AT LIVERY.   LOOSE BOXES.

CHARLES GRAHAM, Proprietor.

The price tariff for horse-drawn vehicles for hire from Charles Graham's West Cliff Mews at the turn of the century. Private transport was not cheap!

Opposite below: The Tally-ho, seen here on 2 October 1913, and the Tantivy were two well-known coaches that provided round trips of the town from The Square.

Cabmen at the Lansdowne (where they had a shelter) with the Misses Chancellor of the Cabmen's Letter Mission.

A splendid picture on the West Cliff showing a donkey-drawn bath chair.

Final days for a variety of competing carriages and omnibuses plying for hire in the Square.
Within a handful of years of this photograph trams were to appear on the roads, providing cheap
public transport for everyman.

Working with Dr Bottomley, the chief of the district ambulance service, W.W. Graham of West Cliff Mews fitted up a vehicle as a travelling ambulance, operating theatre and mobile x-ray outfit during the First World War. It was the first in the country. In 1916 W.W. Graham was given the commission of lieutenant in the Volunteer Motor Transport.

Above: As the Co-op business grew, particularly in the 1920s with dairy and bakery, motor vans replaced the horse and cart and the Cleveland Road garage was augmented by premises in Malmesbury Park Road.

Left: The advent of the trams necessitated the widening of many roads, including Gervis Place. Nos 1 and 2 Westover Villas were demolished and the land occupied here by the wall on the right was incorporated into the road.

Opposite: Bournemouth kept a ceremonial tram, No. 1, for civic use, which is seen here with Ald. J.E. Beale (mayor 1902–1905) in the cab, July 1902. Unlike service trams it was fitted with a plush red carpet and loose basketwork seats.

The tramways provided a number of jobs, not just for drivers and conductors, but also for apprentices straight from school as seen here at Southcote Road tram depot.

There was a splendid waiting room in the centre of the Square (donated by Capt. H.B. Norton in 1925) at a time when there was little danger to pedestrians crossing the road to reach it.

After 1935 the trolleybuses and petrol buses filled the Square. Note that the tram shelter has given way to the clock tower in the middle of a roundabout by 1947.

While being more flexible than the trams (although still restricted to routes fixed by unsightly overhead power lines) trolleybuses could still cause and get caught up in traffic jams, as seen here in the 1950s, looking up Avenue Road towards the Fifty Shilling Tailors. A chocolate and cream Bealeson's van appears to have cut across the bows of a private saloon car and is being approached by an official.

An autumn outing for Beales' staff in Royal Blue charabancs, 1920s. Mr and Mrs Herbert Beale are in the front seats and white-capped drivers marshal the shop worker passengers.

The newly opened (March 1931) bus station in Exeter Road served Hants and Dorset Motor Services Ltd and, on a lower deck, Royal Blue coaches. After severe damage by a fire it was demolished in 1983.

In 1935 this decorated open top bus was entered by Hants and Dorset in the Silver Jubilee Carnival.

A range of motorcars was available for hire from the West Cliff Mews.

Andrews Bros (Bournemouth) Ltd had a good idea that many wish had survived. They offered to wash cars while the owner shopped – avoiding parking charges, which were obviously a pain even in the 1930s!

A tank engine built in 1900 for the LSWR in Southern Railways livery on the turntable outside the sheds at the Bournemouth Goods Yard in May 1940.

A train departs for the west from the central station in 1904.

A new angle on 'trips round the bay'? Sponsored by the *Daily Mail* a seaplane flown by pioneer French aviator Henri Farman landed and was drawn up on the beach, which had been cleared of the public and boats in 1912.

After the aviation meeting of 1910 local meetings were held at various locations. The famous French aviator, M. Hamel, is seen here landing at Meyrick Park in 1914.

Another common landing place was at Wallisdown. Amy Johnson's famous DH Gipsy Moth *Jason* landed here on its penultimate flight when she was visiting Bournemouth in 1930. The plane is now in the Science Museum, London.

In this case the flying field is Ensbury Park Racecourse – an area then in Poole Rural District Council's area, now fully developed by housing. This photograph was taken at the meeting held at Easter 1927. A farmer shot at a low flying aircraft and appeared in court, supported by his friend, the artist Augustus John. Because of protests against Sunday flying and a poor accident record, it was decided after a further meeting at Whitsun that the field was too small for further air races.

The popular heroes of the day were the captains of the paddle steamers plying from both Bournemouth and Boscombe piers, idolised with their own postcards sold to boost the company profits. Another ploy was to take a plate picture of the embarking passengers, as here on the *Emperor of India*, captained by 'Tilsed', 11 August 1913 and then sell souvenir prints as they disembarked after a trip round the Isle of Wight, or to Lulworth Cove, for tea.

The *Balmoral* paddle steamer embarking passengers in 1908 against the background of seaside hotels on the West Cliff, an area now dominated by the Bournemouth International Centre.

Jake 'Ginger' Bolson's cry, of 'Anyone for the *Skylark*?' was a popular one for decades in pre-war days. These sturdy boats were built in the Bolson's Poole shipyard. They embarked passengers off their own jetty alongside Bournemouth pier. The Poole firm played a sterling part in the war effort including building landing craft used in the 1944 D-Day operation.

twelve

Personalities

John Elmes Beale (1848–1928), the
founder of the store bearing his name, lost
his father, a Weymouth sea captain, when
he was a youngster. He worked hard in
retailing in Manchester and Weymouth and
by 1881 had saved enough to open his
own shop in rented premises in fast-
expanding Bournemouth, under the name
of Fancy Fair. It prospered and grew by
acquisitions nearby. The jumble of
premises was rebuilt as an entity in 1923.
The business has been passed on to
successive generations of the family serving
as chairmen or directors until the present
day. A deacon of Richmond Hill
Congregational church, J.E. Beale took
social responsibilities seriously. In 1902 he
was elected Mayor of Bournemouth and
served three terms to 1905, championing
many of the borough's major
improvements, some prestigious, such as
the Undercliff Drive and Pavilion and
others more mundane but still important,
such as the sewerage facilities in Winton.

Charlie Cross was mine host of the Royal
Arms at nos 52-54 Commercial Road, at
the junction with Orchard Lane and Street.
Orchard Street is worth a remark as
Bournemouth's only 'street' – perhaps
thought fitting in days past to its location
next to working class housing. The public
house bordered on one of the most densely
developed working-class areas of
Bournemouth, later demolished as slums,
which had lain hidden behind more
grand façades.

Above: Edith (left) and Ellen Cooper-Dean, whose family had lived in the area for 300 years, and developed the West Cliff and Dean Park areas of the town, opened the Courage public house off Holdenhurst Road at Castle Lane, named after their family, in 1960. Neither sister married and the family is now extinct.

Right: Cumberland Clark was the author of humorous rhymes, of the type that Cyril Fletcher later became famous for, published in the very popular 1929 *Bournemouth Song Book* and thirty-two others; all rather jingoistic. A Yorkshire man who retired to Bournemouth, he had been a great traveller, a sheep drover and a gold miner in his day. He died at Fern Bank, St Stephens Road in a daylight-bombing raid in 1941 and is buried in Boscombe cemetery. Typical lines from his songs are: 'If along the cliff you stroll/Keep your footsteps in control/For you'll come an awful biff/ if you tumble off the cliff./It's a very nasty drop/to the bottom from the top.'

Alderman John Clark Webber (1842
–1924), a classmate of Sir Frederick
Treves, the royal surgeon, and Thomas
Hardy at school in Dorchester, came to
Bournemouth in 1880 as Eldridge Pope's
brewery representative and ran the South
Western Hotel until 1892. In 1890 he was
appointed one of the original
Bournemouth Commisssioners
(predecessors of the Council), later joined
Hampshire CC as well, and was mayor in
1899/1900, becoming the 'Father of the
Council'. His General Omnibus Company
provided public transport before the
tramways. He was also concerned about
the need for Civic buildings and
campaigned for a town hall, law courts
and for the council to take over the
Winter Gardens. In his retirement speech
he said Bournemouth should 'take care of
the band….a great asset to Bournemouth'.
On his death tributes talked of 'his
personality being as outstanding as his
ample figure'.

William Wells Graham OBE (187–1947)
was the founder and general manager of
Hants and Dorset Motor Services. He
worked for his father, Mr C. Graham, at
West Cliff Mews and began running a
private motorcar hire business in 1905. In
1916 the business was turned into a
company – the beginnings of a bus and
coach empire that had 350 vehicles and
1,100 staff by the time he retired in 1945.
In the First World War he fitted up the
first mobile x-ray unit ever used in
England, working in all the military
hospitals. He was a founder member of
Bournemouth Rotary Club, and a former
president of Bournemouth Chamber of
Trade. His sporting prowess included
playing for the Bournemouth Swallows
(predecessor of Bournemouth FC) from
1892, rowing and playing hockey for
Bournemouth Sports Club.

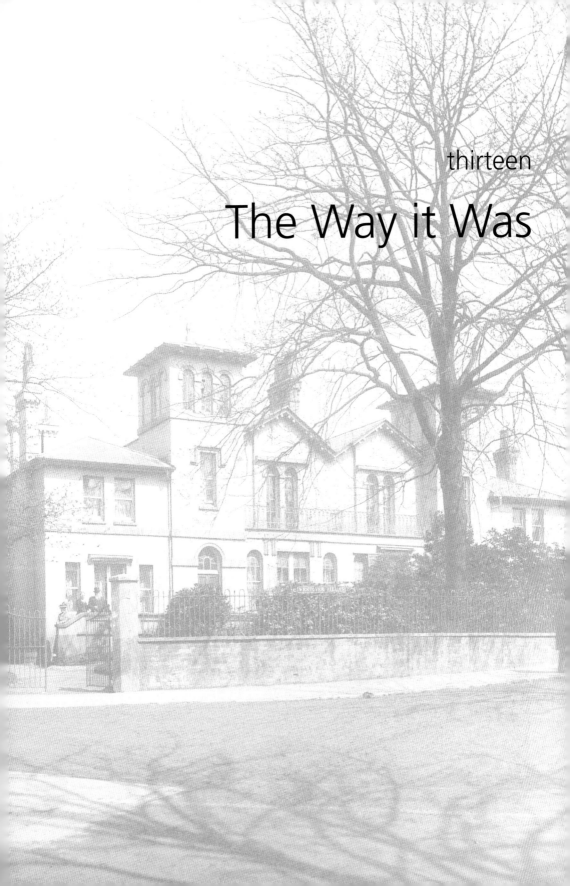

thirteen

The Way it Was

Above: This fine photograph of the late 1890s shows, on the right, nos 1-2 Westover Villas, the original 1860s home in Bournemouth of Henry Mooring Aldridge, a solicitor, and family, who are standing in the doorway. Further along Westover Road, where the cinemas and ice rink are, or were, was Westover Palace. The villas were demolished and redeveloped and this site has been used for the premises of Austin Reed for many years.

Left: Westbourne Congregational church stood at the junction of Poole Road and Prince of Wales Road. The site was redeveloped and is now part of an International Language School. This picture was taken in 1961 when the Fire Brigade assisted in the replacement of the weathercock that had blown down in a storm.

The foot of Richmond Hill and The Square in the early 1870s and St Andrew's Scotch church, built in 1857, which was a galvanised iron structure. Richmond Hill was leafy and undeveloped at that date and was photographed by A. and E. Seely. The bush in the foreground obscures the hut of a rival pioneer photographer, Robert Day! The shops on the right are where W.H. Smith now trade.

The original Winter Gardens pictured here in the early 1900s, was built in 1876. It was filled with potted palms and housed 5,000 people. At first the musical diet was of Italian bands, but from 1892 there was a Corporation Band, at first military, but from 1893, under Dan Godfrey, it became increasingly involved in symphonic work. The 'Cucumber Frame', as the glass structure was affectionately known, was dated and redundant when the Pavilion was opened.

A great attraction to visitors to Southbourne was the shell garden, with mottos, built up by the owner, George Howard, over the years 1948 to 1986. It started as a memorial to a son who died of meningitis. George Howard said, 'Shells are the only thing in the world that grow more beautiful after death'.

The seasonal Fairway caravan park, West Howe, consisted of modern serviced caravans with an electricity supply and hot and cold showers. It was located at Ringwood Road, Northbourne. The site has now been redeveloped for housing.

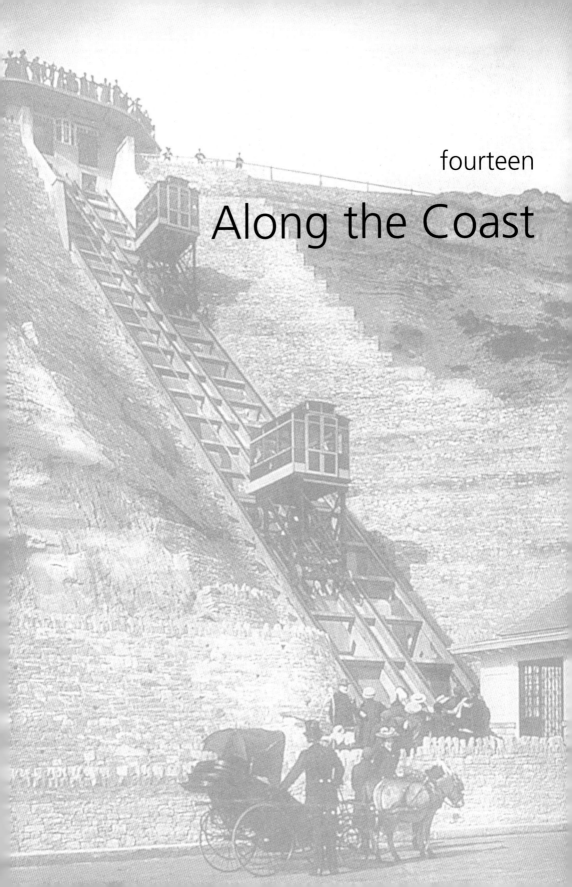

fourteen

Along the Coast

Bournemouth agrees with me Splendidly. The people here vie one with the other In giving Visitors a real good time.

Left: While health and beauty were proclaimed as being available at Bournemouth (the town's motto is *Salubritas et Pulchritido*), the freedoms the beach offered were reflected in this early saucy postcard. Earlier, D.H. Lawrence had once advised, 'Never come here for a holiday – it is more like a hospital'.

Below: This map shows the extent of the development of the town and its attractions in 1873, including the chines and beaches. A chine is a local word found in Hampshire and the Isle of Wight to describe a ravine.

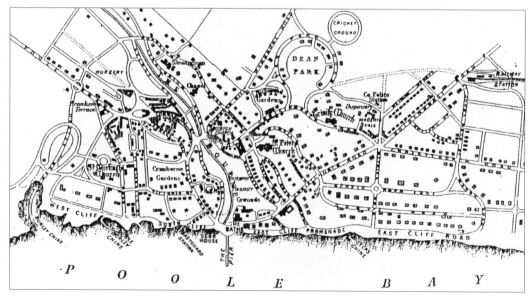

Starting at Alum Chine, the bathing machines, invented in Bath, were wheeled to the margin of the sea to enable women to descend modestly into the briny, suitably clad from neck to toe. The photographer in this photograph from around 1890, borrowed from a private album, has risked his cumbersome equipment to get a rare view from the sea back to the shore.

Members of Bournemouth Natural Science Society (whose centenary was in 2003) are seen on a field visit to Middle Chine in 1912, searching for fossil leaves in the cliffs.

The boundary between Hampshire and Dorset was a bit nebulous in the early days and until Bournemouth transferred to Dorset in 1974 was east of Branksome Dene Chine. In the early 1800s Durley Chine was regarded as the boundary. This 1930s postcard looking towards Sandbanks shows a novel and popular water chute offshore, which featured in the town's tourist guides.

Refreshment facilities soon sprang up in the form of wooden tearooms directly on the beach affording protection from the wind on blustery days, as at Alum Chine. There was no promenade or undercliff, as it is known in Bournemouth, to protect from erosion. In the sixteenth century there had been an unsuccessful attempt to mine copperas (alum) used in the dying and tanning trades, from the chine.

The approach down the bare cliff face to the beach from the heights of the Overcliff was by a zigzag path, lined by Purbeck stonewalls softened by planting and with plenty of elegant seats. This work was done at the same time as the West Cliff beach lift or 'railway' was constructed in the early 1900s. This wartime photograph clearly shows the anti-invasion works just offshore.

A 'monster hotel…under spirited management' was created out of the High Cliff Mansions on West Cliff in 1874, replacing the old coastguard station with the former cottages in the grounds. It would appear from this 1905 photograph that the signalling point on the cliff top was retained. A memorable Labour Party conference was held here in 1940 at which the party agreed to support Churchill's War Cabinet in a government of national unity.

Bournemouth's Rotten Row? A riding school provided instruction in equestrian arts along the safe and level promenade. In 1841 a visitor had written that 'Bournemouth is a very pretty place to look at but not to stay at. We shall not be able to go donkey riding as there are no donkeys to be had.' Donkeys were indeed a rarity on the beaches although ponies were available at some periods.

On the sands near the pier the meticulously crafted and elaborate sand sculptures of J. Suchomlin were an outstanding attraction for many years.

A rare picture of the first pier under construction in 1861. Gas lighting was installed in 1873, but in 1876 around 100 feet of the pier was destroyed in a storm. The Belle Vue Hotel (left) was demolished in 1929 to make way for the Pavilion and the pier approach. It was, until the first synagogue was built, where the Jewish community met for worship. Sydenham, a Poole publisher and bookseller, had established the Royal Marine Library and adjoining baths (centre) as a perfect combination for ensuring the recovery of health of the invalid visitors to Bournemouth.

This photograph comes from the days when you could fish, sail or hire a boat and pull it up the beach by the pier, have your photograph taken and let your children climb the remains of the jetty before strolling to the cliff top to admire the view, without worrying if your parking fee had run out! What you could not do in 1861 when this photograph was taken, was to stroll along the pier – it was yet to be built!

A surprising beach occupant? Peter the Tramp on the Jockey Scales by the Pier Approach Baths, run for many years by the Hurdle family. You could pit your weight against the proprietor's guesstimate. In more recent years, for a wager of £1, a 'guess your age man', the late Lee Bennett, operated at the Pier Approach. He was often accurate and claimed hands gave people's age away but he found teenage girls the hardest to guess.

The Pier was breached in 1939 to discourage enemy landings and in 1947 work began to close the gap and reopen the pier for pleasure boats, pedestrians and fishermen.

The cluttered beach in 1890, viewed from the East Cliff before the construction of the Undercliff. Modern times would surely not allow horses, carts and caravans to be parked freely, unfenced swings to operate and bathing machines at the water's edge to obscure the sea view? It's more like a fairground, but was obviously fun, as was the novelty of walking out to sea on an elegant pier for a few pence, while listening to the sounds of competing rival bands.

On Easter Day 1933 an unbroken stream of 5,000 cars an hour was estimated to be passing to and from the Undercliff Drive in this photograph taken at midday by well known freelance photographer S.W. Batting of Parkstone. He commented that the traffic was actually moving each way – so sea glimpses were possible for the drivers. Louis Tregonwell, the reputed founder of Bournemouth, would not have recognised any of this scene.

Before the Undercliff linked Bournemouth with Boscombe the paths to the east of the pier soon petered out and mountaineering skills were needed by those intrepid and energetic enough to zigzag up the sandy cliffs.

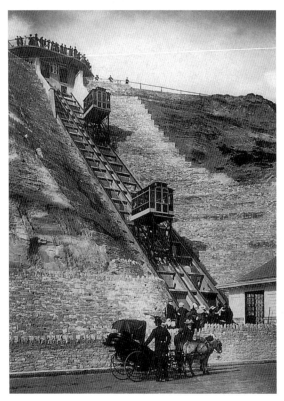

The East Cliff lift was opened by Lady Meyrick in 1908. Sir George Meyrick had given the Corporation rights to build an Undercliff in 1903.

Boscombe Pier, opened in 1889, was built by Sir Henry Drummond Wolff, who aspired to create a rival resort, with a spa, to outperform Bournemouth. It was a private venture costing £12,000 but was not a financial success and was bought by the Corporation in 1903.

Dr Compton's development of Southbourne included a pier, esplanade and a Winter Garden but little now remains to remind the visitor of these ventures. The 300ft pier pictured here was erected at a cost of £4,000 in 1888 by a Poole contractor, Howell of Waterloo Iron Foundry. It was ruined by storms in 1900 and then dismantled as a dangerous structure.

A postcard of old Southbourne showing the remains of the pierhead after the removal of the pier in 1907. The Isle of Wight is visible in the background.

The last addition to the Borough boundaries was in 1930, when the Corporation bought Hengistbury Head (visible on the left) from Gordon Selfridge for £25,250. Hengistbury is a site of great antiquity and significance. It was sold to the London storeowner by Sir George Meyrick, who had planned to build 'the largest castle in the world' with 300 rooms. Fortunately nothing materialised and we are left with this sole barren reminder of the way the rest of Bournemouth's coast looked before the town developed as a coastal resort.

A Bournemouth postcard from the early twentieth century.

Other local titles published by Tempus

Poole The Second Selection
IAN ANDREWS AND FRANK HENSON

This collection of over 200 photographs of Poole take the reader on a nostalgic journey through the town's history. The scenes reflect all aspects of life in Poole over the years; from views of once familiar buildings, shops and firms, to snapshots of local people involved in all manner of work and play activities. There are also interesting features about Poole Town Football Club and Poole lifeboats.
0 7524 1624 3

Bournemouth International Airport
MIKE PHIPP

Bournemouth's links with aviation started with the pioneer aviation meeting in the town in 1910. However it was not until 1941 that Hurn became an RAF station, used for the invasion of Normandy and, briefly, at the end of the war the base became Britain's main civil airport. Mike Phipp tells the story of Hurn from its wartime days right up to the present and shows us the wide variety of aircraft, both military and civil, that have used the one-time RAF base.
0 7524 2396 7

Historic Gardens of Dorset
TIMOTHY MOWL

Until 1900 Dorset remained the semi-feudal society that Thomas Hardy knew, and its gardens relected that. Small manor houses of the sixteenth and seventeenth centuries lay tucked away in downland folds or by winterbourne meadows. Then, in the late twentieth century, a new wave of designers settled in the county creating the historic gardens of the future. This book is calculated to set readers driving off to make their own judgements in our last unspoilt Arcadian county.
0 7524 2535 8

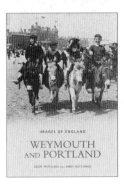

Weymouth and Portland
GEOFF PRITCHARD AND ANDY HUTCHINGS

This book traces some of the developments that have taken place in Weymouth and neighbouring Portland during the last century. Illustrated with over 220 pictures taken by photographer Edwin H. Seward, this volume highlights some of the important events that have occured during this time, including blitz bombing during the Second World War, and the arrival of the railway at the end of the nineteenth century.
0 7524 3066 1

If you are interested in purchasing other books published by Tempus, or in case you have difficulty finding any Tempus books in your local bookshop, you can also place orders directly through our website
www.tempus-publishing.com